Wim Delvoye

Drawings - Scale Models

2000-2005

SPERONE WESTWATER

1

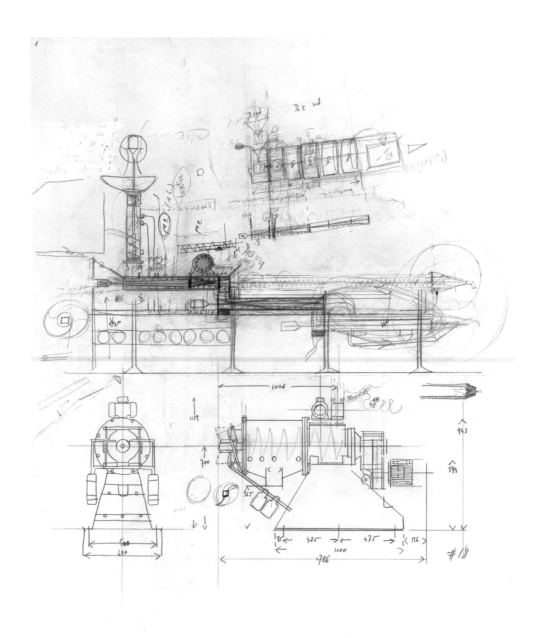

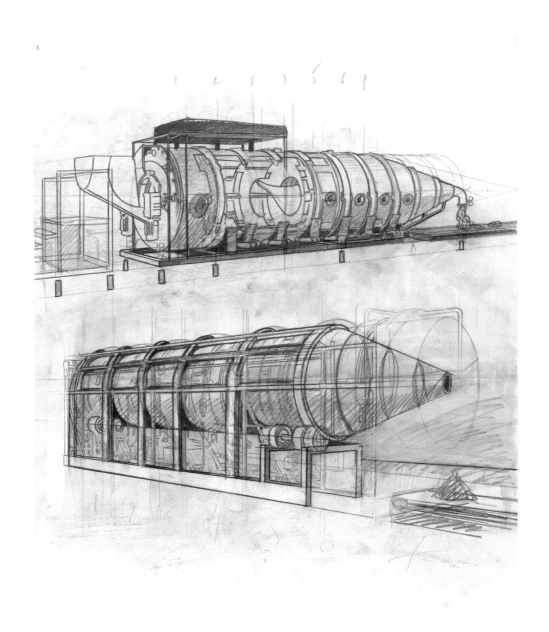

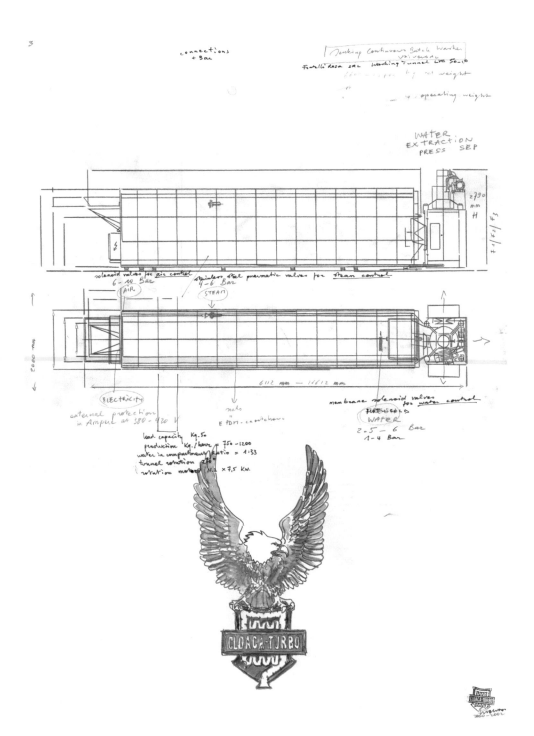

connections
+ Bar

Jenking Continuous Batch Washer
universal
Fratelli Rosa SRL   Washing Tunnel LVE 50-10

~ operating weight

WATER
EXTRACTION
PRESS   SEP

2790
mm
H

solenoid valves for air control
6 - 10 Bar
AIR

stainless steel pneumatic valves for steam control
4 - 6 Bar
STEAM

6112 mm — 14612 mm

ELECTRICITY

external protection
in Ampul at 380 - 420 V

EPDM - caoutchouc

membrane solenoid valves
for water control
HOT COLD
WATER
2.5 — 6 Bar
1 - 4 Bar

load capacity   Kg. 50
production   Kg./hour = 750 - 1200
water in compartment ratio = 1:33
tunnel rotation   2 f.
rotation motors   N.1 × 7,5 Kw.

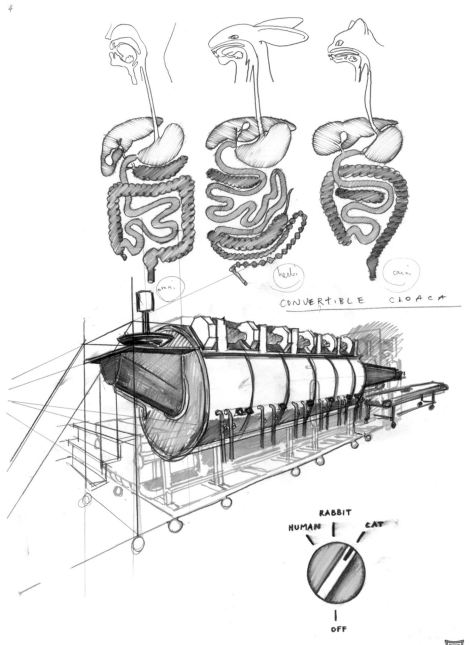

CONVERTIBLE CLOACA

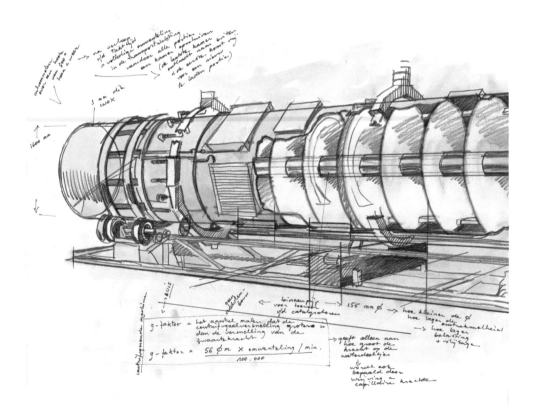

6

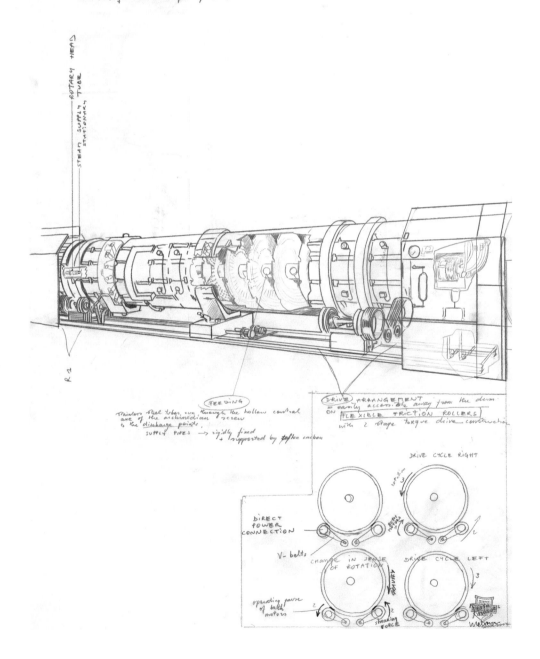

CLOACA - ARCHIMEDIA
single drum batch working system
with controlled batch separation
in a modified contra-flow process

FEEDING

DRIVE ARRANGEMENT

FLEXIBLE FRICTION ROLLERS

DRIVE CYCLE RIGHT

DIRECT
POWER
CONNECTION

V-belts

CHANGE IN SENSE
OF ROTATION

DRIVE CYCLE LEFT

operating pause
of batch
motors

shearing
FORCE

archimedes

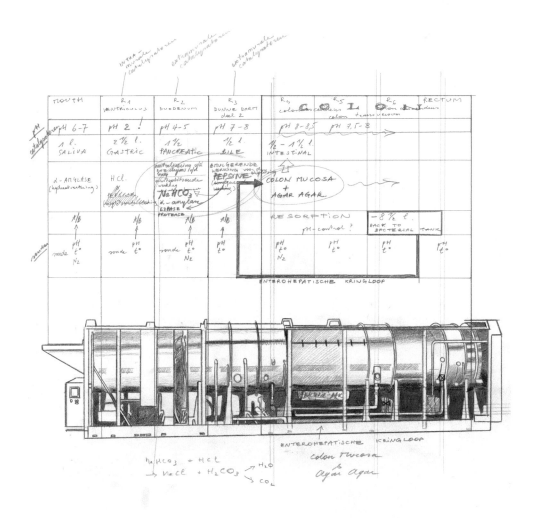

OBLIGATION

CONVERTIBLE

Cloaca

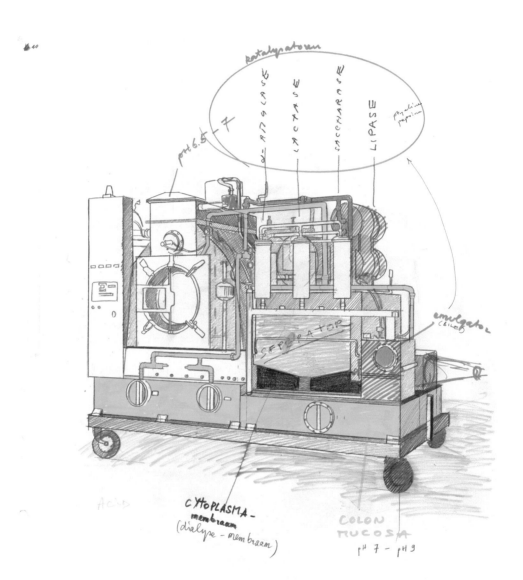

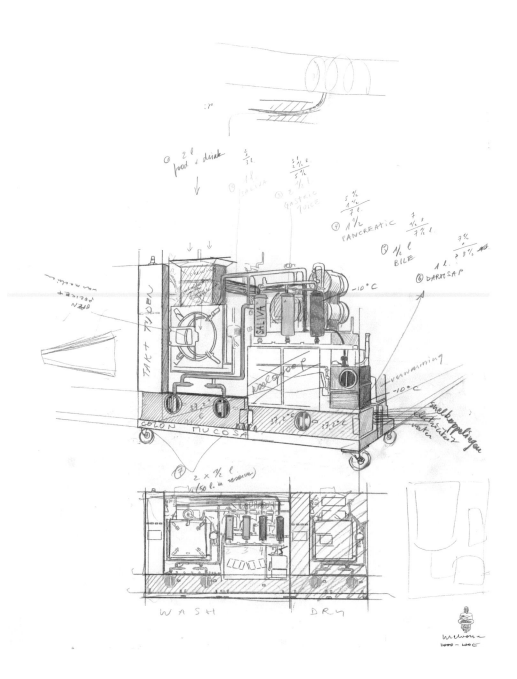

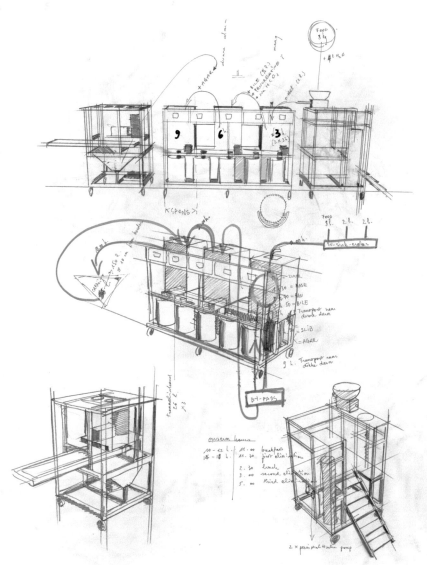

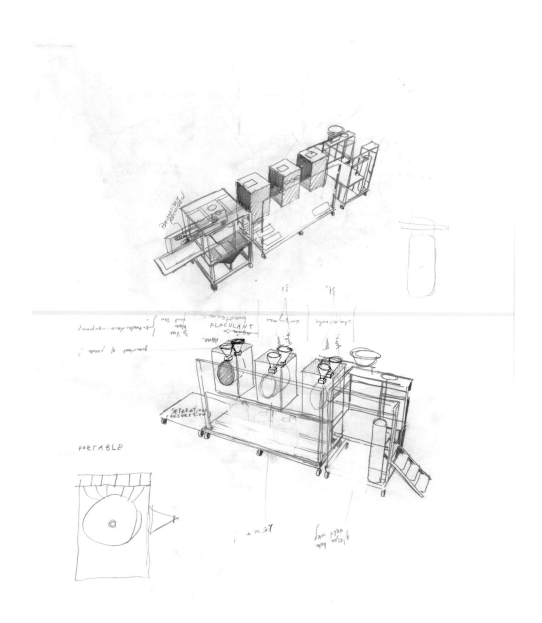

PORTABLE

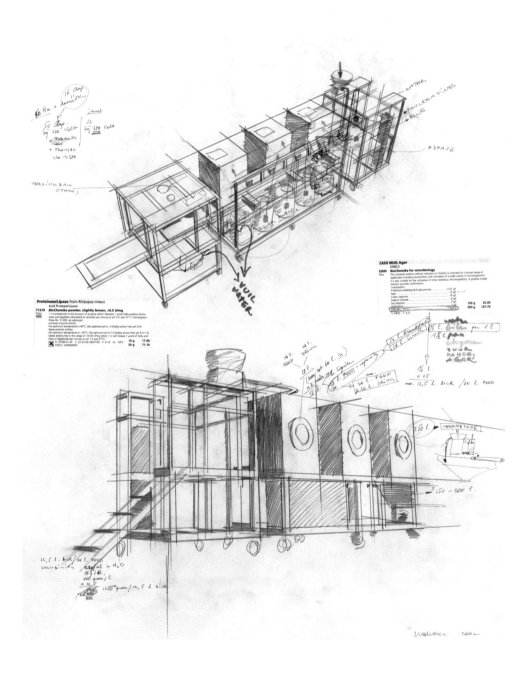

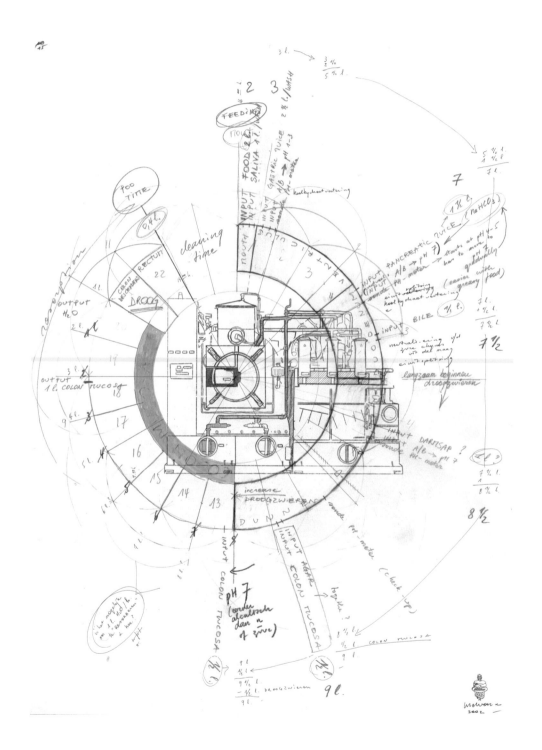

GASPILLA - BACKSIDE

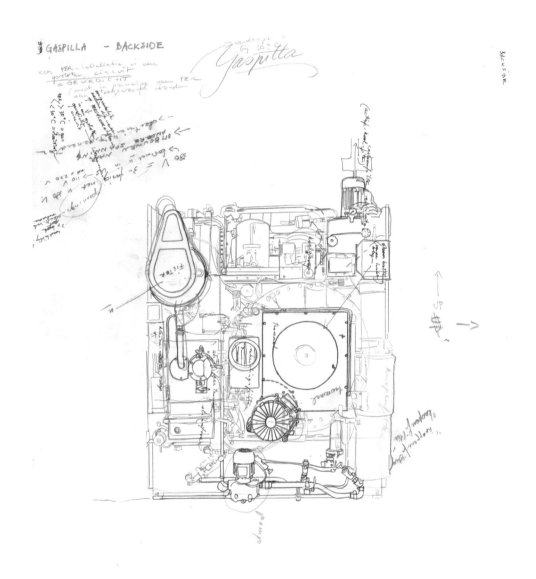

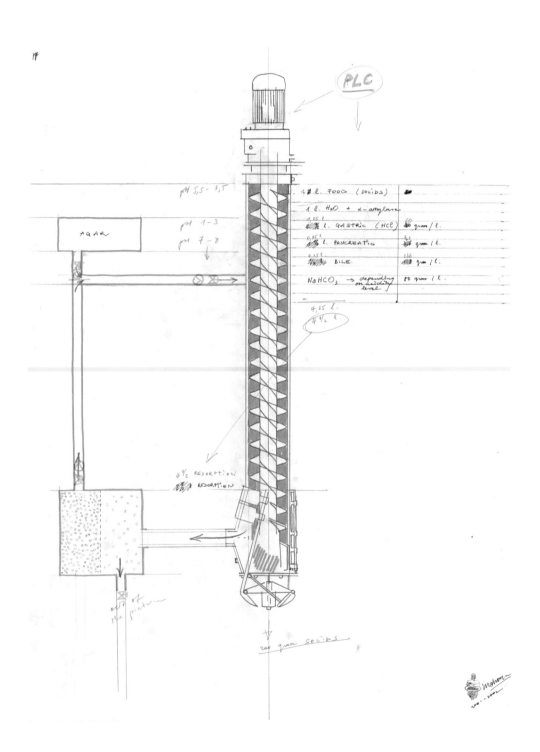

PLC

pH 5,5 - 7,5

AGAR

pH 1-3

pH 7-8

1 l. FOOD (SOLIDS)

1 l. H2O + α-amylase

1,25 l.
2 1/2 l. GASTRIC (HCl)   60 gram / l.

0,25 l.
1 1/2 l. PANCREATIC   2,2 gram / l.

0,25 l.
1 1/4 l. BILE   116 gram / l.

NaHCO3 → depending on acidity level   80 gram / l.

4,25 l.
4 1/2 l.

4 1/2 RESORPTION
8 1/2 RESORPTION

out of the picture

200 gram SOLIDS

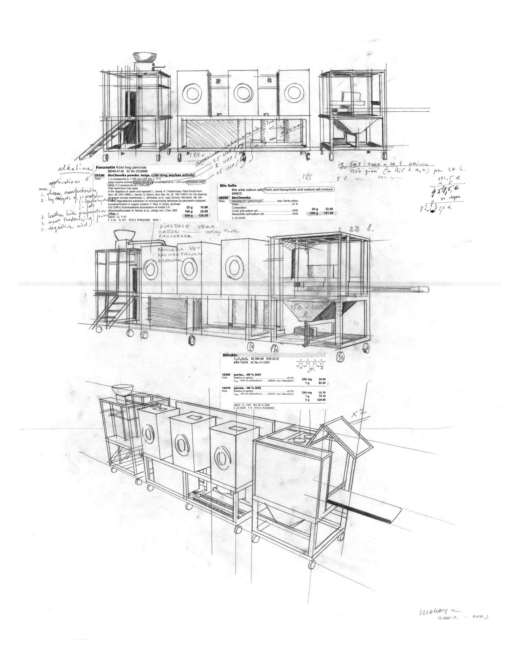

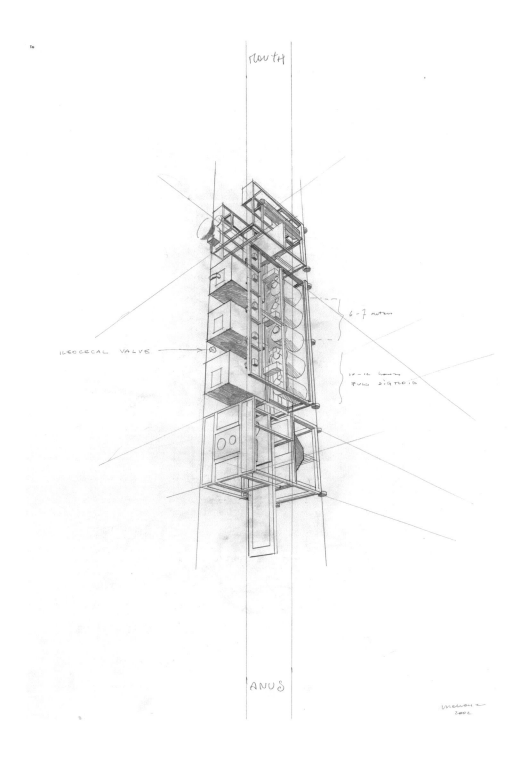

MOUTH

ILEOCECAL VALVE ⟶ ⊗

6 - 7 meters

10 - 12 hours
FULL SIGMOID

ANUS

Melanie
2002

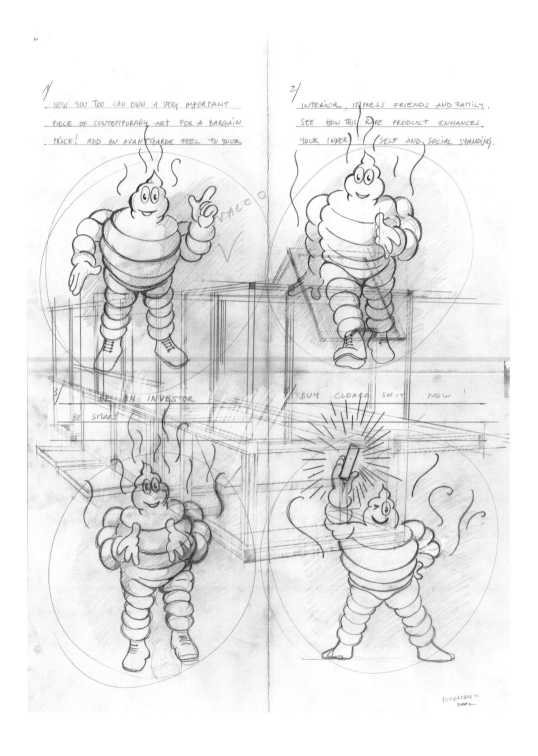

23

THERE IS A MOMENT WHEN YOU BECOME
PART OF TIME.
AND A MOMENT WHEN YOU BECOME
PART OF HISTORY.

SINCE 2000
Cloaca

You never
actually own a Cloaca Shit
You merely
look after it for the next generation.

BUY ONE,
GET ONE free!

② Begin your own tradition.

Cloaca
imagination at work

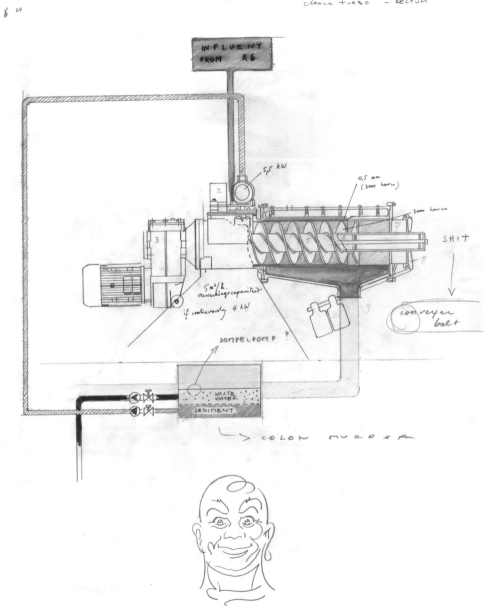

CLOACA TURBO — RECTUM

INFLUENT FROM R6

5,5 kW

0,5 mm (3000 hours)

3000 hours

SHIT

5 m³/h. verwerkingscapaciteit

if continuously 4 kW

conveyer belt

DOMPELPOMP ?

WASTE WATER

SEDIMENT

COLON MUCOSA

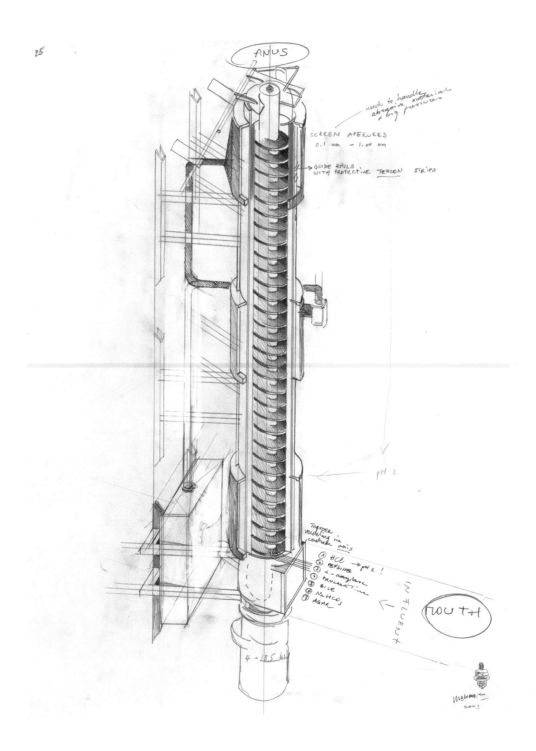

ANUS

needs to handle material
abrasive material
& big pressures

SCREEN APERTURES
0.1 mm - 1.00 mm

GUIDE RAILS
WITH PROTECTIVE TEFLON STRIPS

pH 2

TOEVOER
VERDELING in
centrale as

① HCl → pH 2 !
② PEPSINE
③ L - amylase
④ PANCREATINE
⑤ BILE
⑥ NaHCO₃
⑦ AGAR

INFLUENT

MOUTH

4 - 18,5 kW

Melrose
2003

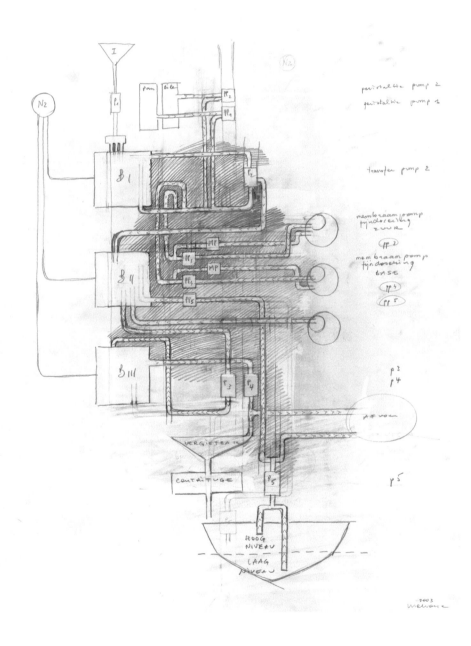

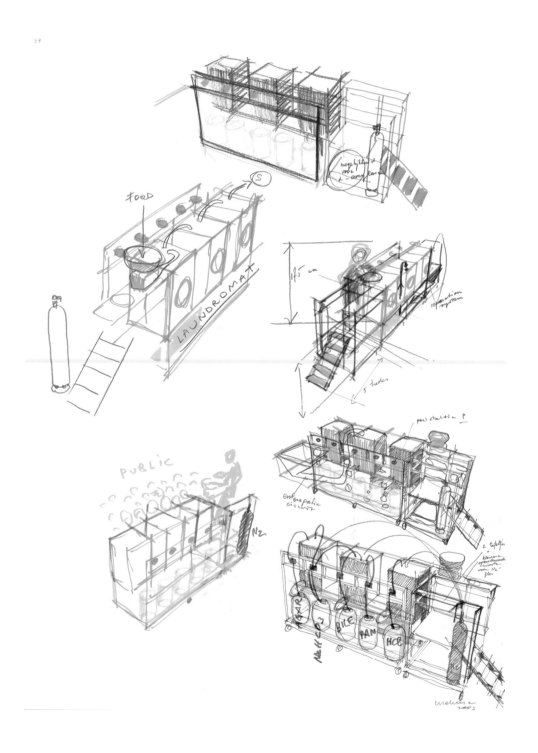

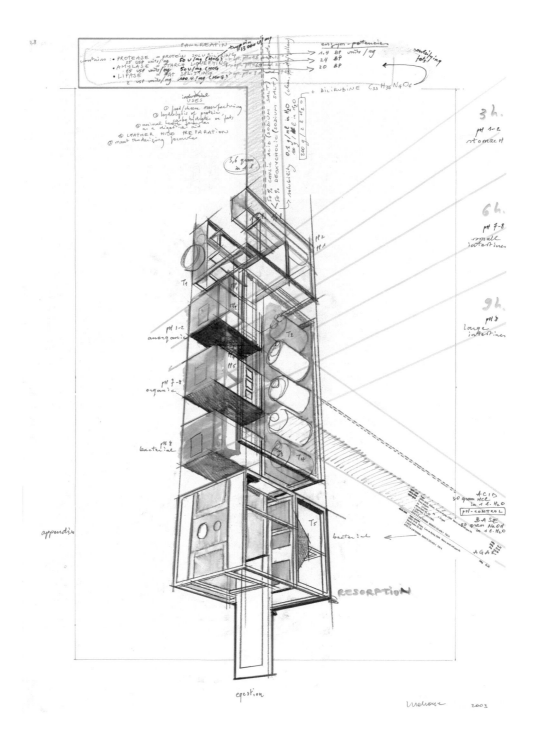

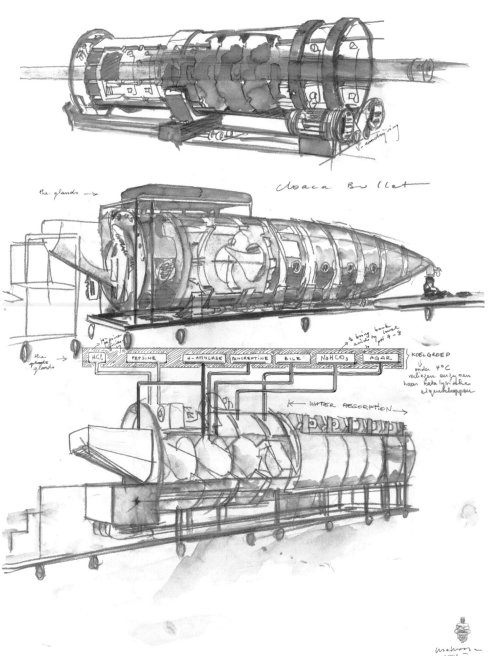

the glands →

Cloaca Bullet

HCL | PEPSINE | α-AMYLASE | PANCREATINE | BILE | NaHCO₃ | AGAR

KOELGROEP
onder 4°C

← WATER ABSORPTION →

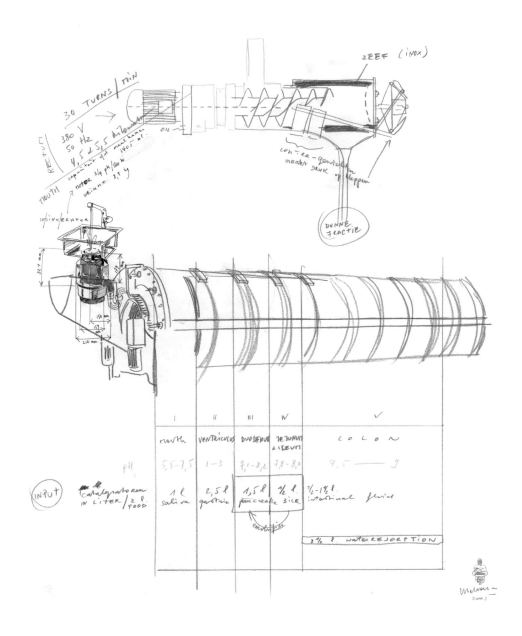

RECTUM ⊃ MOUTH (1)

	I	II	III	IV		V	
	mouth	VENTRICULUS	DUODENUM	JEJUNUM ILEUM		C O L O N	
pH	5,5-7,5	1-3	7,1-8,2	7,8-8,0		7,5 ———— 9	
INPUT catalysatoren IN LITER / 2 ℓ FOOD	1 ℓ saliva	2,5 ℓ gastric	1,5 ℓ pancreatic	½ ℓ BILE	½-1½ ℓ intestinal fluid		
						8½ ℓ. WATER RESORPTION	

CLOACA TGQ

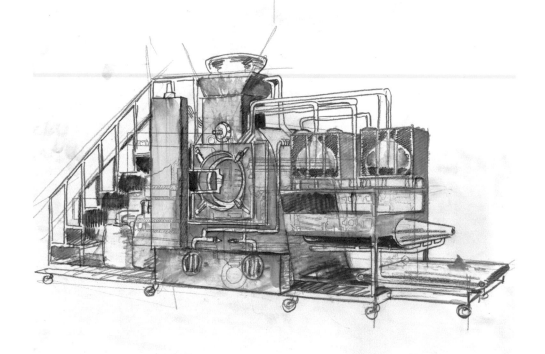

32

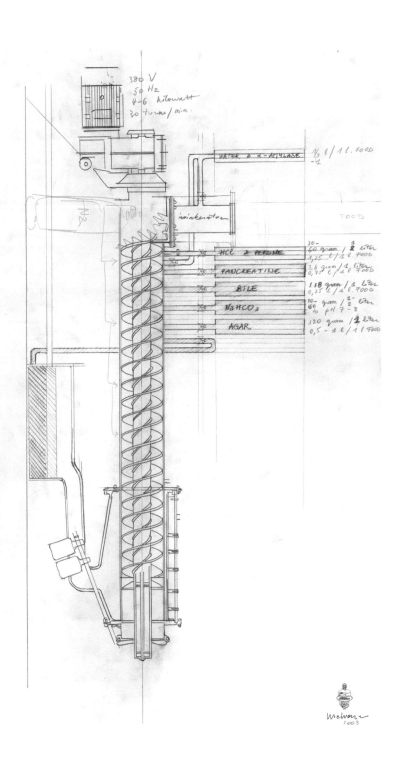

380 V
50 Hz
4-6 kilowatt
30 turns/min.

WATER & ɑ-AMYLASE   1/8 ℓ / 1 ℓ. FOOD
                    -1/4

incinerator

FOOD

HCL & PEPSINE   30-
                 60 gram / 1/2 liter
                 1,25 ℓ / 1 ℓ. FOOD

PANCREATINE   3,6 gram / 1 liter
                 0,75 ℓ / 1 ℓ FOOD

BILE   118 gram / 1 liter
                 0,25 ℓ / 1 ℓ. FOOD

Na HCO₃   10- gram / 1- liter
                 160   / 2
                 to pH 7 - 8

AGAR   120 gram / 1 liter
                 0,5 - 1 ℓ / 1 ℓ FOOD

Mehwa
2003

33

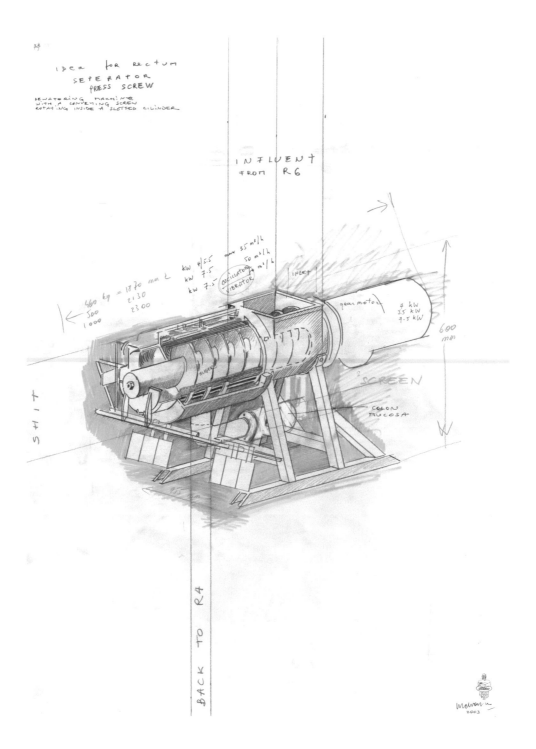

idea for rectum
SEPERATOR
PRESS SCREW

DEWATERING MACHINE
WITH A CONVEYING SCREW
ROTATING INSIDE A SLOTTED CILINDER

INFLUENt
FROM R6

460 kg = 1870 mm L
500   2130
1000   2300

kW 4/5.5   max 55 m³/h
kW 7.5   50 m³/h
kW 7.2   40 m³/h

OSCILLATOR
VIBRATOR

INLEt

gear motor

4 kW
5.5 kW
7.5 kW

600
mm

SCREEN

COLON
MUCOSA

AUGER

SHIT

BACK TO R4

Melvan
2003

34 IDEA FOR A RECTUM

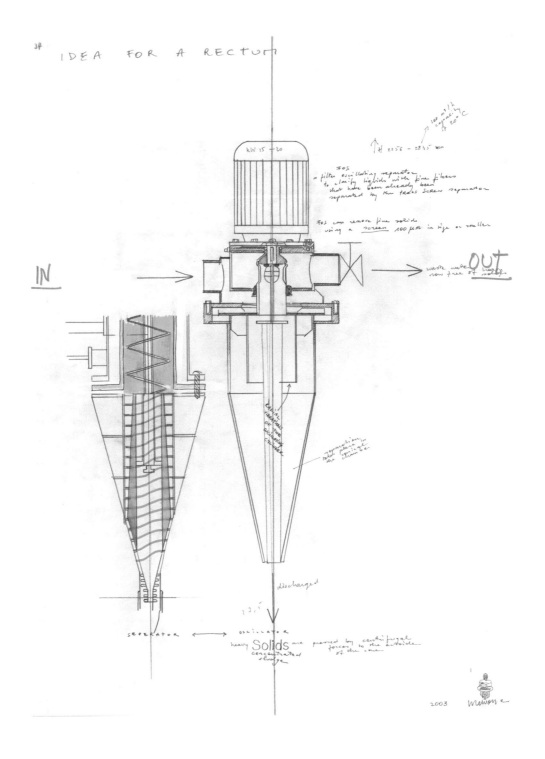

IN →

OUT

2003 mewone

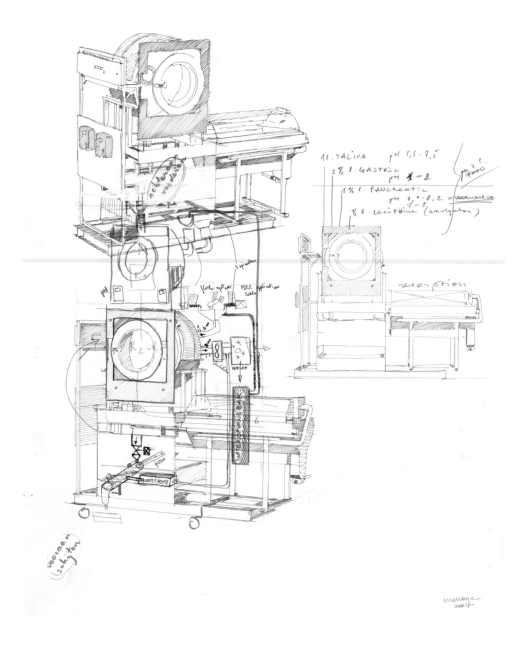

1 l. SALIVA   pH 5,5-7,5
2½ l. GASTRIC   pH 1-8
1½ l. PANCREATIC   pH 7,1-8,2 = VOORWARMDE
½ l. lecithine (emulgator)

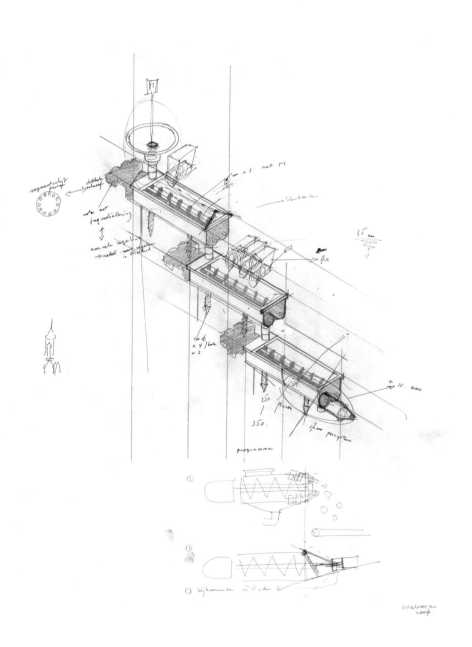

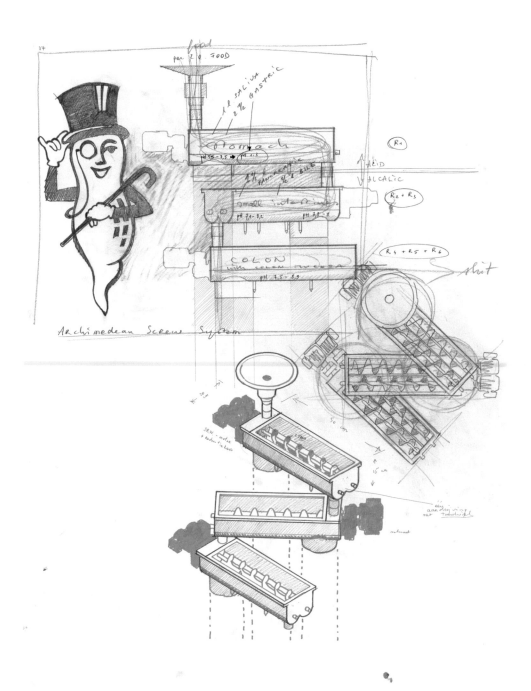

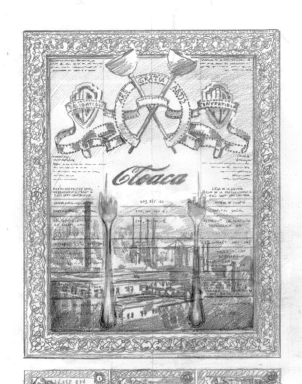

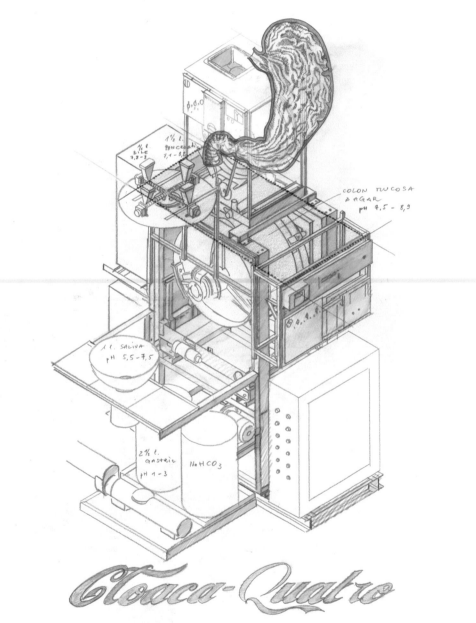

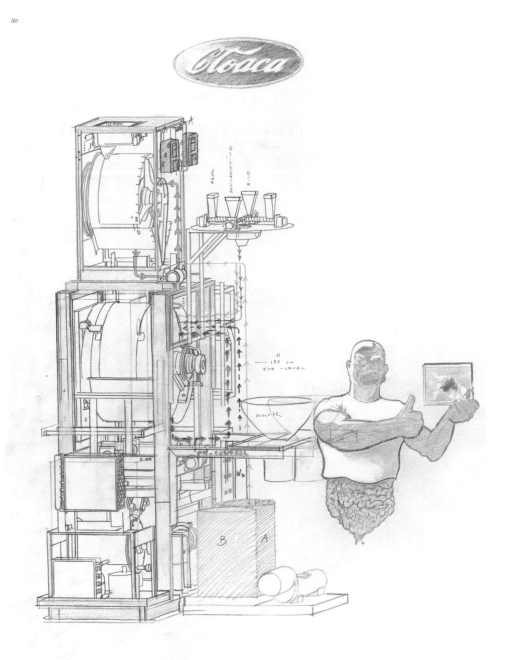

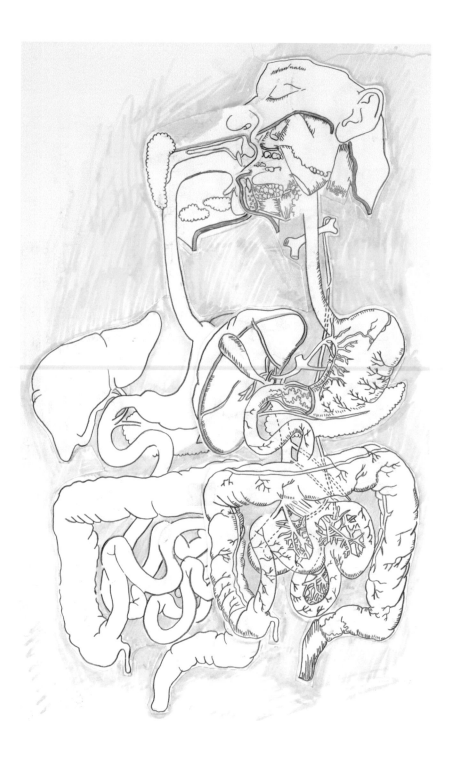

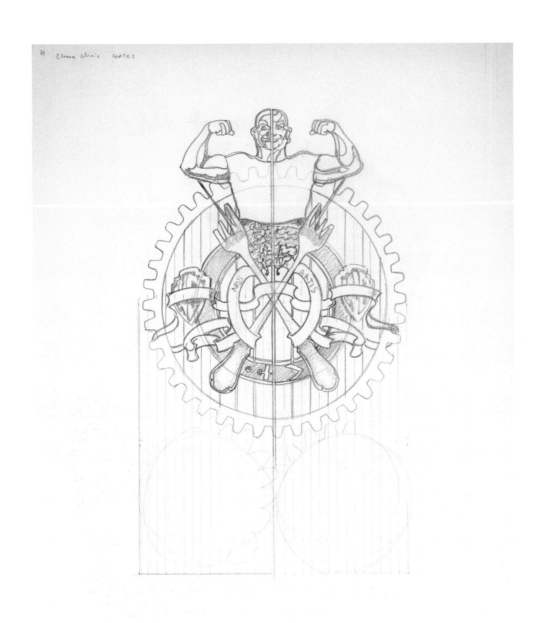

45

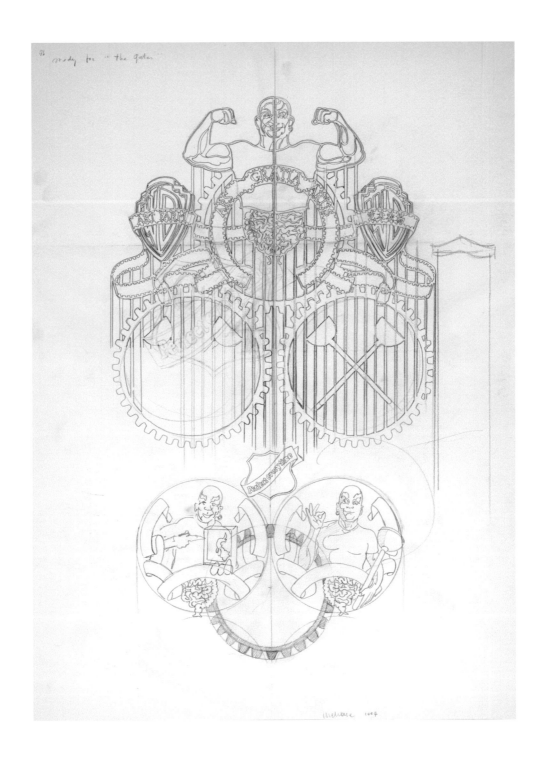

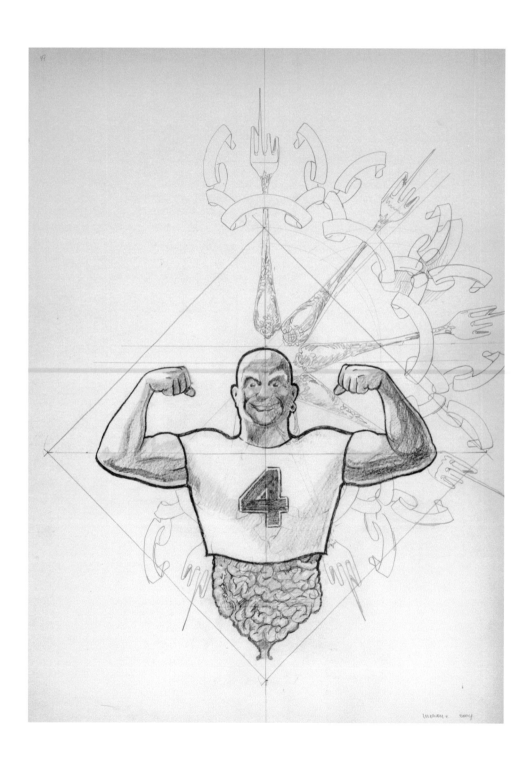

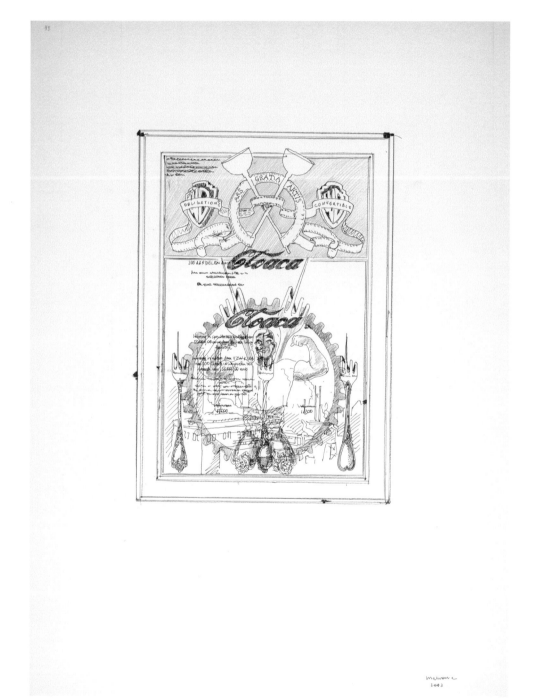

49

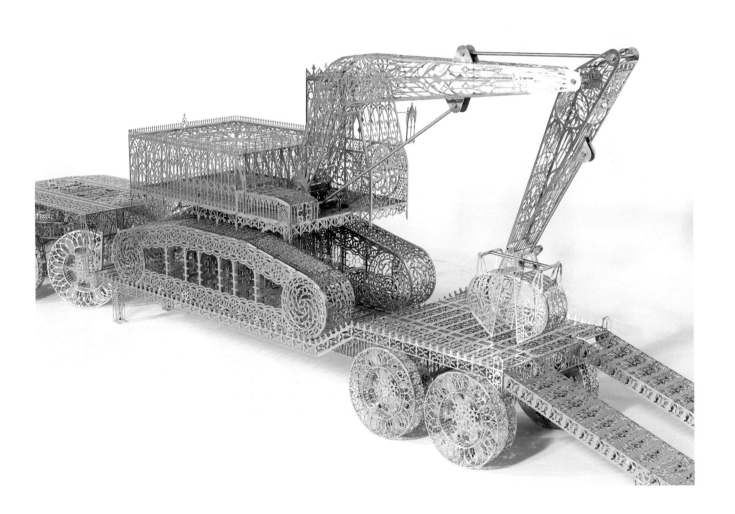

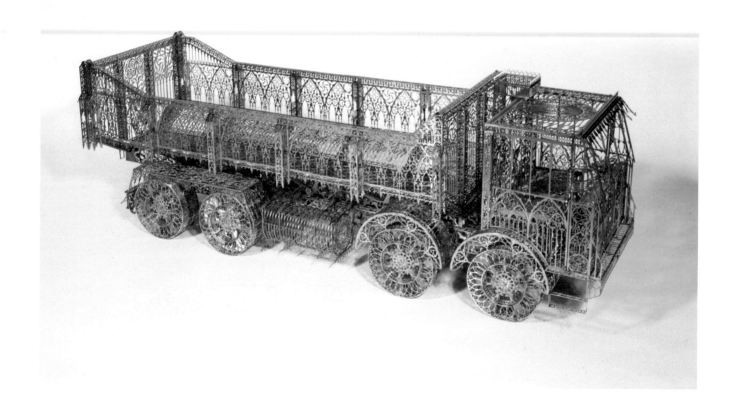

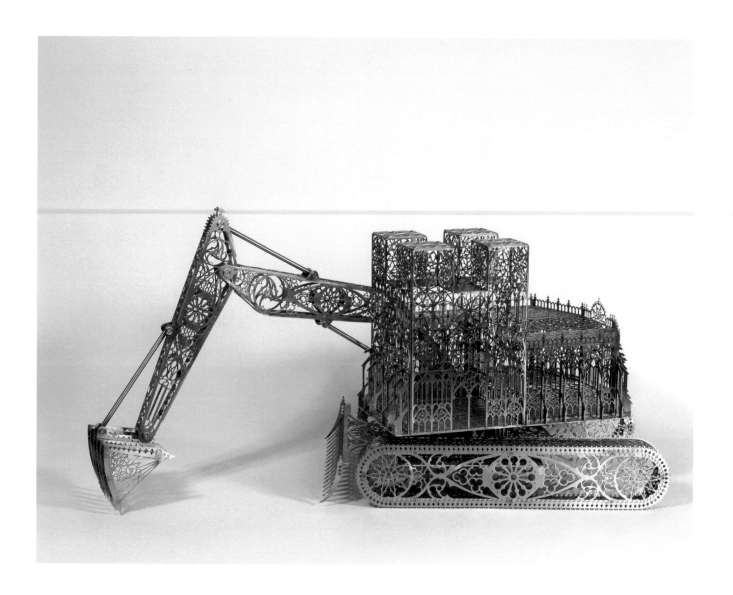

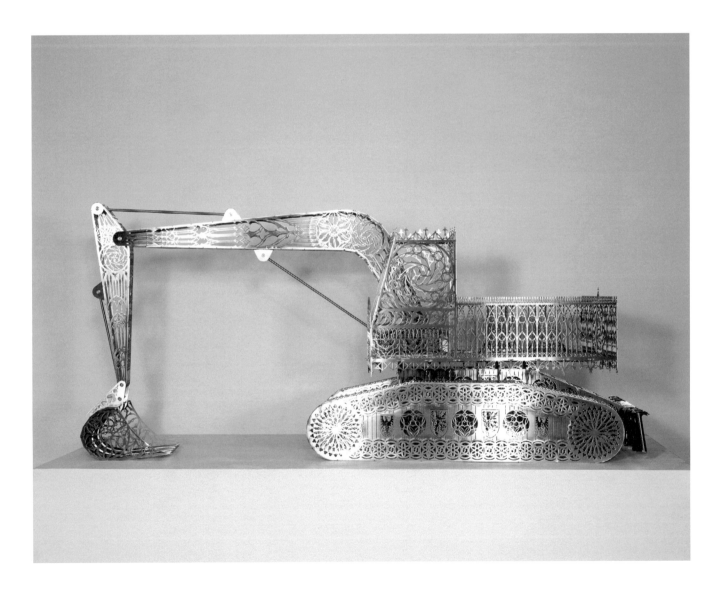

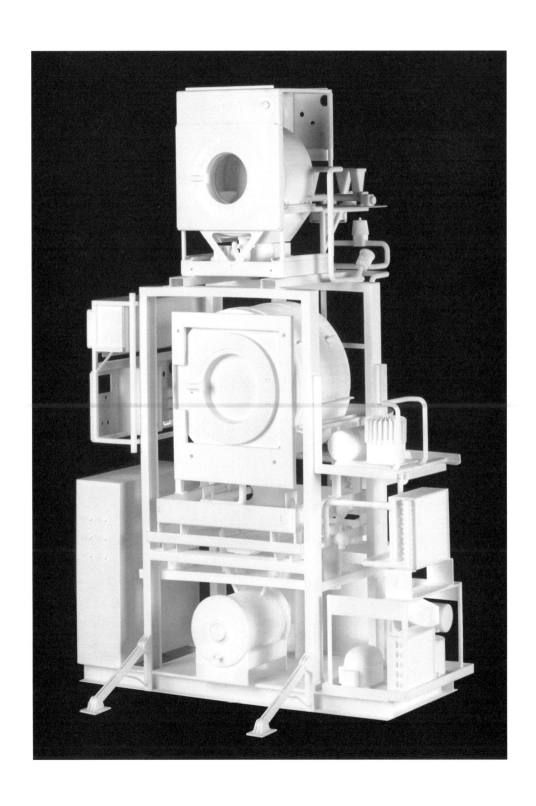

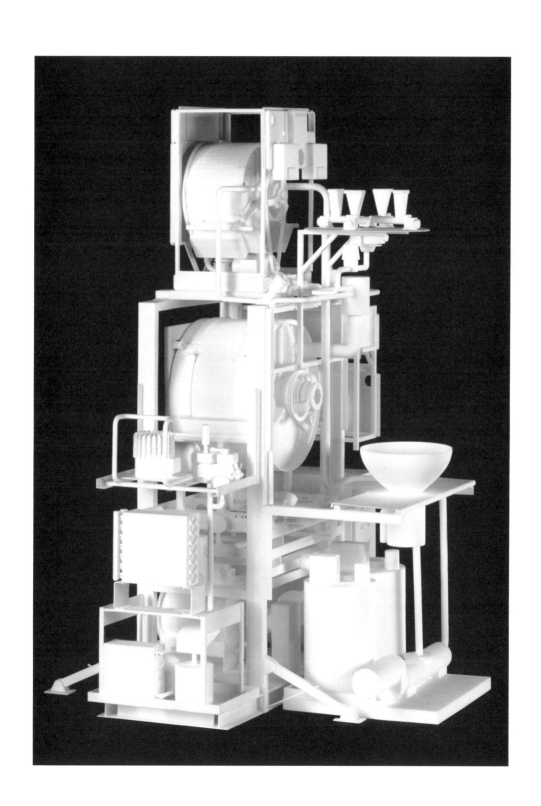

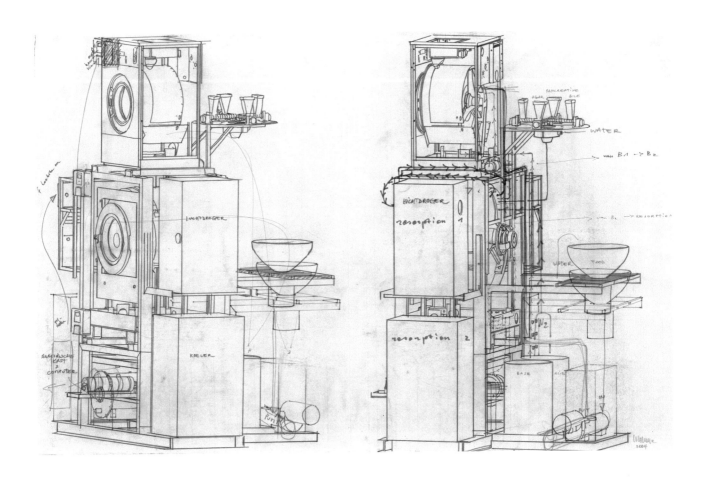

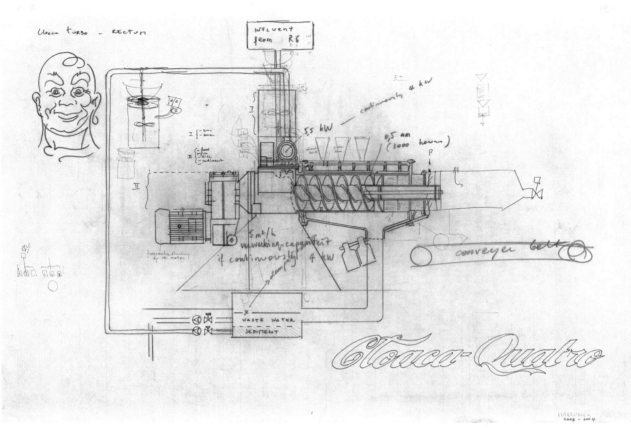

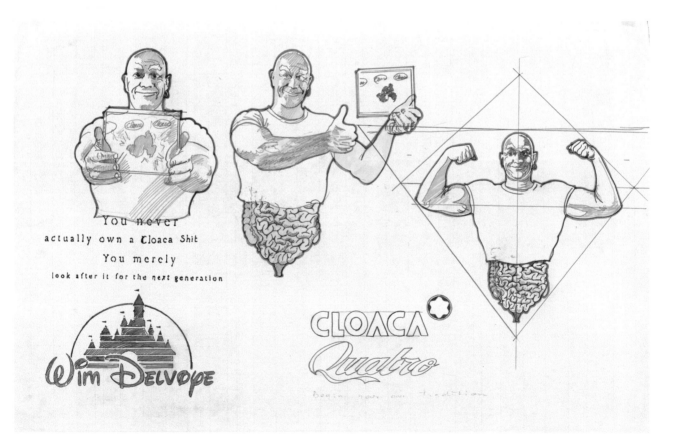

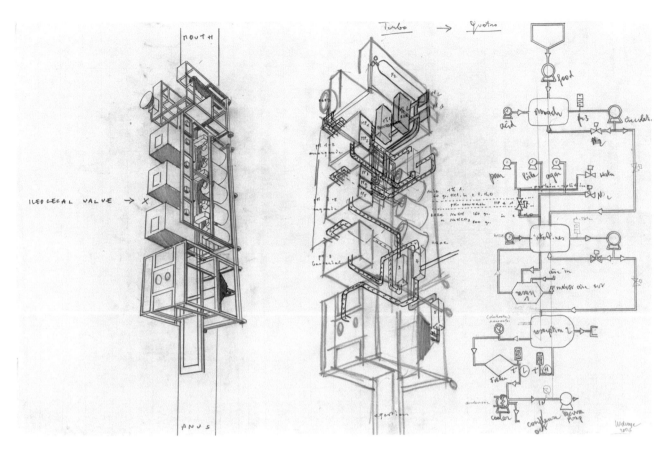

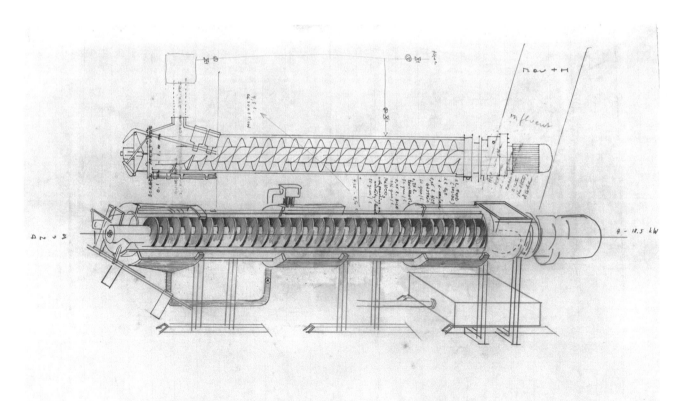

LIST OF WORKS

1   DRAWING #1 (2000), COLOUR PENCIL, PENCIL, MARKER ON PAPER, 21 7/8 x 29 5/8 INCHES [55,5 x 75,5 CM]

2   DRAWING #2 (2000-2001), COLOUR PENCIL, WATERCOLOUR ON PAPER, 21 7/8 x 29 5/8 INCHES [55,5 x 75,5 CM]

3   DRAWING #3 (2000-2001), COLOUR PENCIL, WATERCOLOUR ON PAPER, 21 7/8 x 29 5/8 INCHES [55,5 x 75,5 CM]

4   DRAWING #4 (2000-2002), PENCIL, MARKER ON PAPER, 21 7/8 x 29 5/8 INCHES [55,5 x 75,5 CM]

5   DRAWING #5 (2000-2002), COLOUR PENCIL, MARKER, WATERCOLOUR ON PAPER, 21 7/8 x 29 5/8 INCHES [55,5 x 75,5 CM]

6   DRAWING #6 (2000-2002), COLOUR PENCIL, PENCIL ON PAPER, 21 7/8 x 29 5/8 INCHES [55,5 x 75,5 CM]

7   DRAWING #7 (2000-2002), COLOUR PENCIL, MARKER ON PAPER, 21 7/8 x 29 5/8 INCHES [55,5 x 75,5 CM]

8   DRAWING #8 (2000-2002), COLOUR PENCIL, PENCIL, MARKER ON PAPER, 21 7/8 x 29 5/8 INCHES [55,5 x 75,5 CM]

9   DRAWING #9 (2001), COLOUR PENCIL, PENCIL ON PAPER, 21 7/8 x 29 5/8 INCHES [55,5 x 75,5 CM]

10   DRAWING #10 (2000-2001), COLOUR PENCIL, MARKER ON PAPER, 21 7/8 x 29 5/8 INCHES [55,5 x 75,5 CM]

11   DRAWING #11 (2000-2002), COLOUR PENCIL, PENCIL, MARKER ON PAPER, 21 7/8 x 29 5/8 INCHES [55,5 x 75,5 CM]

12   DRAWING #12 (2002), PENCIL, MARKER ON PAPER, 21 7/8 x 29 5/8 INCHES [55,5 x 75,5 CM]

13   DRAWING #13 (2002), PENCIL, MARKER ON PAPER, 21 7/8 x 29 5/8 INCHES [55,5 x 75,5 CM]

14   DRAWING #14 (2002), PENCIL, MARKER, STICKER ON PAPER, 21 7/8 x 29 5/8 INCHES [55,5 x 75,5 CM]

15   DRAWING #15 (2002), COLOUR PENCIL, PENCIL, MARKER ON PAPER, 21 7/8 x 29 5/8 INCHES [55,5 x 75,5 CM]

16   DRAWING #16 (2002), COLOUR PENCIL, PENCIL, MARKER ON PAPER, 21 7/8 x 29 5/8 INCHES [55,5 x 75,5 CM]

17   DRAWING #17 (2001-2002), PENCIL, MARKER ON PAPER, 21 7/8 x 29 5/8 INCHES [55,5 x 75,5 CM]

18   DRAWING #18 (2002), PENCIL, MARKER, WATERCOLOUR ON PAPER, 21 7/8 x 29 5/8 INCHES [55,5 x 75,5 CM]

19   DRAWING #19 (2000-2003), PENCIL, MARKER, STICKER ON PAPER, 21 7/8 x 29 5/8 INCHES [55,5 x 75,5 CM]

20   DRAWING #20 (2002), PENCIL, MARKER ON PAPER, 21 7/8 x 29 5/8 INCHES [55,5 x 75,5 CM]

21   DRAWING #21 (2002), COLOUR PENCIL, PENCIL ON PAPER, 21 7/8 x 29 5/8 INCHES [55,5 x 75,5 CM]

22   DRAWING #22 (2000-2003), COLOUR PENCIL ON PAPER, 21 7/8 x 29 5/8 INCHES [55,5 x 75,5 CM]

23   DRAWING #23 (2003), PENCIL ON PAPER, 21 7/8 x 29 5/8 INCHES [55,5 x 75,5 CM]

24   DRAWING #24 (2003), PENCIL, MARKER, WATERCOLOUR ON PAPER, 21 7/8 x 29 5/8 INCHES [55,5 x 75,5 CM]

25   DRAWING #25 (2003), PENCIL, MARKER ON PAPER, 21 7/8 x 29 5/8 INCHES [55,5 x 75,5 CM]

26   DRAWING #26 (2003), PENCIL, MARKER ON PAPER, 21 7/8 x 29 5/8 INCHES [55,5 x 75,5 CM]

27   DRAWING #27 (2003), PENCIL, MARKER ON PAPER, 21 7/8 x 29 5/8 INCHES [55,5 x 75,5 CM]

28   DRAWING #28 (2003), COLOUR PENCIL, PENCIL, MARKER, STICKER ON PAPER, 21 7/8 x 29 5/8 INCHES [55,5 x 75,5 CM]

29   DRAWING #29 (2003), PENCIL, MARKER, WATERCOLOUR ON PAPER, 21 7/8 x 29 5/8 INCHES [55,5 x 75,5 CM]

30   DRAWING #30 (2003), COLOUR PENCIL, PENCIL, MARKER, TAPE ON PAPER, 21 7/8 x 29 5/8 INCHES [55,5 x 75,5 CM]

31   DRAWING #31 (2003), PENCIL, WATERCOLOUR ON PAPER, 21 7/8 x 29 5/8 INCHES [55,5 x 75,5 CM]

32   DRAWING #32 (2003), COLOUR PENCIL, PENCIL ON PAPER, 21 7/8 x 29 5/8 INCHES [55,5 x 75,5 CM]

33   DRAWING #33 (2003), COLOUR PENCIL, PENCIL, MARKER ON PAPER, 21 7/8 x 29 5/8 INCHES [55,5 x 75,5 CM]

34   DRAWING #34 (2003), PENCIL, MARKER ON PAPER, 21 7/8 x 29 5/8 INCHES [55,5 x 75,5 CM]

35   DRAWING #35 (2004), COLOUR PENCIL, PENCIL, MARKER ON PAPER, 21 7/8 x 29 5/8 INCHES [55,5 x 75,5 CM]

36   DRAWING #36 (2004), PENCIL, MARKER ON PAPER, 21 7/8 x 29 5/8 INCHES [55,5 x 75,5 CM]

37   DRAWING #37 (2004), COLOUR PENCIL, PENCIL, MARKER ON PAPER, 21 7/8 x 29 5/8 INCHES [55,5 x 75,5 CM]

38   DRAWING #38 (2004), COLOUR PENCIL, PENCIL, MARKER ON PAPER, 21 7/8 x 29 5/8 INCHES [55,5 x 75,5 CM]

39   DRAWING #39 (2004), COLOUR PENCIL, PENCIL, WATERCOLOUR, MARKER ON PAPER, 21 7/8 x 29 5/8 INCHES [55,5 x 75,5 CM]

40   DRAWING #40 (2004), COLOUR PENCIL, PENCIL, MARKER ON PAPER, 21 7/8 x 29 5/8 INCHES [55,5 x 75,5 CM]

41   DRAWING #41 (2000), COLOUR PENCIL, PENCIL, MARKER, COLLAGE ON PAPER, 21 7/8 x 29 5/8 INCHES [55,5 x 75,5 CM]

42   DRAWING #42 (2003-2004), COLOUR PENCIL, PENCIL ON PAPER, 21 7/8 x 29 5/8 INCHES [55,5 x 75,5 CM]

43   DRAWING #43 (2004), COLOUR PENCIL, PENCIL ON PAPER, 21 7/8 x 29 5/8 INCHES [55,5 x 75,5 CM]

44   DRAWING #44 (2004), COLOUR PENCIL, PENCIL ON PAPER, 21 7/8 x 29 5/8 INCHES [55,5 x 75,5 CM]

45   DRAWING #45 (2004), COLOUR PENCIL ON PAPER, 21 7/8 x 29 5/8 INCHES [55,5 x 75,5 CM]

46   DRAWING #46 (2004), COLOUR PENCIL ON PAPER, 21 7/8 x 29 5/8 INCHES [55,5 x 75,5 CM]

47   DRAWING #47 (2004), COLOUR PENCIL ON PAPER, 21 7/8 x 29 5/8 INCHES [55,5 x 75,5 CM]

48   DRAWING #48 (2003), COLOUR PENCIL, PENCIL, MARKER ON PAPER, 21 7/8 x 29 5/8 INCHES [55,5 x 75,5 CM]

49   DRAWING #49 (2004), COLOUR PENCIL ON PAPER, 21 7/8 x 29 5/8 INCHES [55,5 x 75,5 CM]

50   DRAWING #50 (2004), COLOUR PENCIL ON PAPER, 21 7/8 x 29 5/8 INCHES [55,5 x 75,5 CM]

Solo Exhibitions

1990   Jack Tilton Gallery, New York

1991   Sonnabend Gallery, New York
Art Gallery of New South Wales, Sydney
Castello di Rivoli, Rivoli, Torino

1992   Kunsthalle Nürnberg, Nürnberg
Galerie Micheline Szwajcer, Antwerp
Sonnabend Gallery, New York
Ruth Bloom Gallery, Los Angeles

1993   Galleria Tucci Russo, Torino
Galerie Ghislaine Hussenot, Paris
Galerie Lehmann, Lausanne

1994   Galerie Beaumont, Luxembourg
Center for the Arts, San Francisco, California

1995   Galleria Sperone, Rome
Galleria Cardi, Milan
Gallery Tanit, München
Musée Départemental de Rochechouart, Limoges

1996   Galerie Ghislaine Hussenot, Paris

1997   Open Air Museum Middelheim, Antwerp

1998   Sonnabend Gallery, New York

1999   Galleria Sperone, Rome
Galerie Ghislaine Hussenot, Paris
FRAC des Pays de la Loire, Nantes
Galerie Micheline Szwajcer, Antwerp
Galerie Laura Pecci, Milan

2000   Cement Truck, Centre Georges Pompidou, Paris
Galerie Krinzinger, Vienna
CLOACA, MuHKA, Antwerp

2001   *Cloaca - New & Improved*, Migros Museum, Zürich

2002   Galerie Nathalie Obadia, Paris
Cloaca - New & Improved, New Museum, New York
Museum Kunst-Palast, Düsseldorf
Marble Floors, Sperone Westwater, New York
Porin Taidemuseo, Pori (Finland)
Gothic Works, Manchester City Art Galleries, Manchester
Gothic Works, Sperone Westwater, New York

2003   Musée d'Art Contemporain, Lyon
Gothic, Public Art Fund Project, New York
Fabrica, C-Arte, Prato

2004   *Cloaca - New & Improved*, The Power Plant, Toronto
Oeuvres sur Papier 1968 - 2004, Galerie Obadia, Paris

2005   *Drawings & Scale Models*, Sperone Westwater, New York
Long March Foundation, Beijing
Dolun Museum of Modern Art, Shanghai

Group Exhibitions

1990   *Aperto, Biennale di Venezia*, Venice
Belgique, une nouvelle génération, FRAC de la Loire, Clisson
Confrontaciones, Museo Espanol de Arte Contemporaneo, Madrid
Kunstenaars van Vlaanderen, Museum van Hedendaagse Kunst, Ghent

1991   *Desplazamientos*, Centro Atlantico de Arte Moderno, Las Palmas
Altrove, Museo di Arte Contemporanea, Prato

1992   *Documenta IX*, Kassel
9th Biennial of Sydney, Sydney
Post-Human, Musée d'Art Contemporain, Lausanne /
Castello di Rivoli, Rivoli / Deste Foundation,Athens

1993   *Post-Human*, Deichtorhallen, Hamburg

1994   *EV+A Invited*, Limerick
Depois de Amanha, Lisboa 94, Centro Cultural de Belèm, Lisboa
Cocido y Crudo, Museo Reina Sofia, Madrid

1995   *ARS 95*, Museum of Contemporary Art, Helsinki
Issues of Empire, Guggenheim Gallery/Chapman University, Orange CA

1996   *Everything that's interesting is new / The Dakis Joannou Collection*, Athens
Sammlung Sonnabend. Von der Popart bis heute, Deichtorhallen, Hamburg
Interzones (Copenhagen 96), Kunstforeningen, Copenhagen
Under Capricorn (Art in the Age of Globalisation), Stedelijk Museum,
Amsterdam

1997   *Kwangju Biennale*, Kwangju, South-Korea.
Biennale de Cétignie, Cétignie, Montenegro

1998   *Spatiotemporal*, Magasin 3 Konsthall, Stockholm
Baroque, The Slovak National Gallery, Bratislava
The Summer of 1998, Het Domein, Sittard (the Netherlands)

1999   *De opening*, SMAK, Ghent
L' Envers du Décor, Institut d' Art contemporain, Villeurbanne
Ruralia, Porin Taidemuseo, Pori (Finland)

48th Biennale di Venezia, d' APERTutto, Venice
Zeitwenden - ausblick, Kunstmuseum Bonn, Bonn
Dehors - dedans, Musée d'Art contemporain de Bordeaux,
Bordeaux

2000   *Dust & Dirt*, Witte Zaal, Ghent
Over the Edges, SMAK, Ghent
Partages d' exotisme, 5ième Biennale de Lyon, Lyon
American Bricolage, Sperone Westwater, New York

2001   *Give and Take*, Victoria and Albert Museum, London
Eine Barocke Party, Kunsthalle Wien, Vienna
Confidences, Casino Luxembourg, Luxemburg
The Silk Purse Project, Arnolfini, Bristol
Irony, Fondaçion Mirò, Barcelona
Sonsbeek 9 - LocusFocus, Arnhem (the Netherlands)
Un Art Populaire, Fondation Cartier pour l'Art Contemporain, Paris
Marking the Territory, Irish Museum of Modern Art, Dublin
Sense of Wonder, Herzliya Museum of Art, Herzliya (Israël)

2002   *Melodrama*, Artium, Vitoria-Gasteiz (Spain)
From Pop to Now, Tang Teaching Museum, New York
To Whom it may Concern, CCAC Wattis Institute, San Francisco

2003   *Extra*, Swiss Institute, New York
No Canvas, Galleria Cardi, Milano
GNS, Palais de Tokyo, Paris
Scatalogue, SAW gallery, Ottawa (Canada)
Outlook - Cultural Olympiad, Benaki Museum, Athens

2004   *Settlements*, Musée d'Art Moderne, Saint-Etienne
Giants - Den Haag Sculpture 2004, Den Haag
Continental Breakfast - 45th October Salon, Belgrade
Hors d'Oeuvres - Ordres et désordres de la nourriture, CAPC, Bordeaux

2005   *Visionary Belgium - C'est arrivé près de chez vous*, Bozar, Brussels
8th Biennial of Contemporary Art, Lyon

Acknowledgements

Wim Delvoye would like to thank everyone who helped to contribute to this show, the catalogue and the production of the works: Sabine Castelein, Bart Cloet, Cravero BVBA (Thierry & Carla Verroeye, Monique De Craemer, Dirk De Groote and the rest of the team, for their special efforts), Cassochrome (Bernard & Laurence Soens), Gianni Degryse, Wouter De Winter, Frank Eulaers, Piet Lelieur (for his dedication), Dirk Pauwels, Karen Polack, Michael Short and Royce Weatherly. A special word of gratitude, for their loyal support of Wim Delvoye's work, goes out to Sperone Westwater (David Leiber, Gian Enzo Sperone & Angela Westwater), Mr Mickey Cartin, Public Art Fund (Susan K. Freedman, Tom Eccles & Richard Griggs), Mr Jerry Speyer, and The Walker Art Center.

Published in 2005 on the occasion of the exhibition
Wim Delvoye: Drawings and Scale Models
at Sperone Westwater,
February 25 - March 26, 2005

Designed by Wim Delvoye & Sabine Castelein
Typesetting by Sabine Castelein
Copy editing by Gianni Degryse
Printed by Cassochrome, Waregem, Belgium
Bound by Sepeli, Evergem, Belgium

Photography
Dirk Pauwels: fig. 51, 52, 53, 54, 55
Bart Cloet: fig. 56, 57

info@cloaca.be
info@speronewestwater.com
ISBN: 9080721727
D/2005/10.472/5

FRONTCOVER: 2004 'MR.CLOACA'   BACKCOVER: 1995 'FUCK YOU'